BUT MORE SO

But More So

Samuel Hazo

PITTSBURGH:
Serif Press
2025

Pictured on the cover is Mary Anne Hazo attending one of the
International Poetry Forum's programs.

For those who make a fool of time.

BUT MORE SO

Contents

Part I

In a Few Words

World news is rarely new.
We see, hear or read it
    under different names and let it
    lure us from attention to distraction.
We say it keeps us up
    to date before we're out
    of date.
            That likens it
    to gossip headlined or screened.
Poems do the opposite
    by slowing us down.
               And so
    do single lines that mean more
    than they say like a foreigner's
    last goodbye ("I see you again
    never...") or Jane's reason
    for marrying Joe ("No other
    man could make me laugh...")
    or why Ed makes his own
    furniture ("Wood talks to me...")
What slows us even more
    is letting nothing say everything
    when there's nothing else to say.

Now Then

At my age I see myself
    as past until I learn
    that everybody sees himself
    that way.
              It makes me fret
when I forget the names
of friends or quote my social
security number as my date
of birth.
              Classmates from sixty
years ago say "glad you're still
around."
              I try recalling
who they were from who
they say they are...
              Alone
at home, I listen to Julia's
anthems in Arabic or read
"Mathios Pascalis Among
The Roses" by Seferis.
                  They praise
the sanity of staying put...
Last night I dropped and left
    a penny spinning on the floor.
It demanded that I pick it up.
I refused.

Today it seems
at home where it had spun
and flattened.

No more demands.

Postwarriors

The number of marines killed
   since Korea?
              From Tonkin
   to Fallujah the count is more
   than fourteen thousand for no
   known reason but conquest
   laundered as self-defense.
In addition, more than seven
   thousand veterans kill
   themselves each year.
              Not fit
   for poetry, you say?
              Homer
   and Wilfred Owen—both poets—
   thought otherwise and said so.
Strangers in uniform continue
   killing total strangers
   with even more lethal weapons.
Photos and quotes of generals
   survive—MacArthur wading
   ashore in Leyte like Caesar—
   Curtis Lemay vowing
   to bomb Cuba back
   to the Stone Age.
             The lone
   exception is George C. Marshall—

the first Five Star General,
Chief of Staff, Nobel
Awardee for the Marshall Plan
and Secretary of State.

He warned
Truman that naming Israel a state
would cause continual wars.
He told Johnson that Vietnam
was a mistake.

Unwilling
to profit from the deaths of soldiers,
he refused millions to write
his memoirs...

Born in Uniontown
south of Pittsburgh, he was known
to the older generation simply
as Mr. Marshall or George.

The Time of Day

"Nothing human is alien to me."

Terence

Rebels who refuse to yield
  prevail even in defeat.
Colonists proved that in Boston.
Negritude is still the name
  for black defiance in France.
Florence Nightingale lamented
  the waste of women in society
  and the waste in war of men.
Total war and slaughters
  like Waterloo and D-Day
  are dated and done, but who
  can say the Song of Songs
  or Michelangelo's David
  or the voice of Enrico Caruso
  recorded in his prime are ever
  done?
      What lives forever
in the present has no history
but now.
      It could be art
or music or something we create
or a chosen love remembered.

Somehow, these outlive the loss
    of three million Vietnamese
    plus fifty-five thousand Americans
    decades before we endured
    the hoax of Iraq followed
    by the sight of swaddled infants
    being starved to death in Gaza.
We listen to lies disguised
    as news while trying to remember
    when every day was more
    than just another number.

Guernica

The pope sees genocide in Gaza.
His bishops say nothing, but students
   side with him in demonstrations
   world-wide.
            Invoking
self-defense, the murderers
   of thirty thousand children
   swear they had no choice.
The corporate networks flash
   such news between commercials
   for Kleenex.
          There's no Picasso
   to liken Gaza to Guernica.
A client state controls
   the news.
         The murdered are blamed
   for being murdered.
           Beneath denial
   and deceit, the script's the same.
Whatever will be left of Gaza
   is Guernica with a different name.

Where's Gaza?

With war in the next room
    it's difficult to keep dancing.
But many dance, regardless,
    while clapping in time and singing.
Death does not deter them—
    not even the deaths of children
    bombed.
           They say that death
takes the pleasure out of life,
and pleasure is what they live
to feel.
         All those children
wrapped in sheets for burial
do not exist for them.
They say tomorrow's children
    will replace them soon
    enough.
          Meanwhile, they wonder
why we just ignore such good
music?
       Why?
           For what?

Too Much

Satisfaction troubles me.
                                    Dining
   on shrimp scampi, I say
   I'll stop when I've had enough.
I rarely stop until enough
   becomes too much.
                                    That's how
   satisfaction differs from perfection.
Perfection knows excess at sight
   but often chokes when propaganda's
   hyped and swallowed whole...
Convicted of a felony, a Prime
   Minister addressed Congress
   as an honored invitee.
                                    Many
   called that far from perfect
   and refused to attend...
                                    In Gaza
   a hundred children were bombed
   to bits.
                        The Minister blamed
the children.
                        Citing fake facts,
   he lied to applause.
                                    Nothing

could irk or shame the applauders
while those not applauding smirked.

The Gamble of Nations

Delegations of chauffeured grifters
    meet in Paris, Oslo or elsewhere.
Their rhyming diction teems
    with abstract nouns spoken
    in the passive voice.
                  Each
    participant prattles on of peace,
    but war is hiding in the pauses,
    waiting.
            All in all,
    this mimics the logic of poker
    ruled by the luck of the deal.
Hidden in the deck, the aces
    of extinction lurk to make
    real what's unsaid but likely.

Unthinkable

Asked what he thought of when
    he danced, Michael Jackson
    answered, "Thinking is the enemy
    of dancing."
                My son agreed
  and called that true of all
  the arts.
           Jackson danced
  his footfalls free of forethought.
Even he could not foresee
    what he would do until
    he did it...
               Ask a drummer how
  he drums, and he'll just tap
  a tempo on a table-top.
                  Ask
  a poet how or why his poem
  happened, and you'll wait
  forever.
             Reason understands
  itself.
          Imagination speaks
  from silence to silence.
                 Think
  how algebra differs from poetry.
Algebra's learners stay on the page.

Poetry lives wherever it's read
    or said, and the page keeps turning.

The Moment

It could be sudden as a pause,
    a touch, a sense of nearness
    or a sound.
                 It's not foretold.
Unless it comes unplanned
    and unexpectedly as love, it's best
    ignored.
           But coming from within
    where anywhere and everywhere
    are instantly nowhere but here,
    the moment's never done.
It lets you feel reborn
    the way a poem is reborn
    each time you think it's over
    like a song that keeps singing
    long after it's sung.

Paired

I

You, Aunt Kak and my brother
    Bob made life complete.
Later our son and Dawn
    and their three children
    made it even more so—
    not more but more so.
                Daily
    we hoped such days would last
    although we knew the limits
    in advance.
           Today I write
these words in grateful protest,
knowing how happiness
that happened once demands
to happen twice—but more so.

II

For sixty years we ate breakfast
    at this table together.
              We created

each other to start the day
Now I sit alone.
                    I fill
a glass with cold water
and leave the faucet open.
The water keeps running
    to keep me company.
                        Suddenly
    the phone rings.
                    It changes me
    to someone on demand.
                            It orders me
    to leave the table and answer—
    to leave you.
                    I let it ring.

Rejoinders

I

We seem convinced that life
    reborn as art endures
    in perpetuity.
                Nothing could be
further from the truth.
                  If life
means living breath by breath,
    we live as long as we can breathe.
We live the fullest when
    we're moved to breathe our feelings
    into words.
              We stay alive
in what we've said to those
who've heard us.
              Often
that's perpetuity enough
to tell the living from the dead.

II

Hamlet to his credit kept
    his anguish to himself until

he had no choice.
                              His only
    options were revenge as ordered
    from the grave or swordplay
    he would not survive.
                              His last
    soliloquy was silence...
Romeo and Juliet, like Hamlet,
    had no destiny but love.
They could not live apart,
    and feuding families made
    their lone alternative a sentence.
They faced the doom of hope
    that put them to the test.
                              Unable
    to touch while living on,
    they died together at their best.

To Publish or Perish

"The heart is a more reliable organ than the
brain."

Page Smith

For the ambitious, teaching seems
    nothing but a chore while research
    and publication promise rank
    and status.
            The plan is totally
    corporate.
            Tenure is the goal
since tenure means less time
to teach but time enough
to make a name for yourself
as a scholar, provost or dean
    with special access to the president.
Teaching underclassmen
    can be left to junior faculty,
    graduate assistants and nomads.
But students never can forget
    those few professors who quietly
    chose to teach and share
    their thoughts and doubts with them.
Some will name their very sons
    after them and cherish moments

of silent tribute to them
at class reunions.
                    As for
the rest with their private deals
and titles?
                    They published and perished.

Zero Almighty

Simply considered as digits,
    all zeros amount to nothing.
But adding zeros to whole numbers
    can heighten the final sum
    to millions, billions, trillions.
It made all Europe spurn
    the numerals of Rome in favor
    of nothing.
                Hucksters and thieves
    relied on zeros to measure
    their losses and gains.
                Budgets
of kingdoms functioned the same.
It let the Arabs foresee
    that one-through-nine-plus-zero
    had nowhere but onwardly
    upward or downward to go.

Taps

Poets from Homer onward
   saw wars as times of necessary
   murder.
         Generals like Patton
disagreed, but Brady's photographs
at Gettysburg together with Capa's
on Omaha Beach confirm
how force made worse what might
made right.
         From Troy to Vietnam
killers murdered killers on land,
at sea or in the sky.
         Nothing
but weaponry ruled and foretold
how millions of targets would die.

Bored Meeting

Informed that military suicides
   had averaged twenty-two
   per day since 2016,
   one senator blamed the vets.
A four-star general added,
   "It's not affected enlistments."
"Canada has an assisted suicide
   program that can be accessed
   by Americans," said the Secretary
   of Defense, "so that's an option."
"If suicide is just a more personal
   way of dying," he continued,
   "it needs a different preparation,
   and there's nothing immoral in that."
With nothing better to say,
   they all shook hands and left.

Part II

Destinations

A different man ago
   I could be dared or suckered
   into trips.
         Now I'm constantly
going where I've been, and here
becomes there when I leave.
What prompts me to keep going?
Am I like Eric the Red
   who named Greenland Greenland
   as a lure for settlers to go there?
Does naming let us learn
   we're more than dust, though
   unto dust we shall return?
Or is it simply so
   that going always gives us
   something new to know.
And that is why we go.

Hollyworld

Spangler Arlington Brugh
    became Robert Taylor.
Betty Jean Peske
    turned into Lauren Bacall,
    and Rita Hayworth left
    Margarita Carmen Cansino
    to yesterday forever.
This was Hollywood's way
    (with one or more R's)
    of making actors' names
    sound eternally perfect.
Movie czars believed
    a name's not what you make
    of it but what it makes
    of you.
             And it worked
    as charm and fakery have
    always worked with facts.
Cary Grant succeeded
    Archie Leach.
             Gary
    replaced Frank Edward
    but kept Cooper.
             Greta
    Gustaffson translated
    as Greta Garbo.

It's hard
to admit yet, thanks to the R's,
not a problem to say.
The ultimate exception?
Frederich Meshilem
        Meier Weisenfreund
        shrank to Paul Muni.

Unexpectedly So

I broomed away white dust
   pretending to be snow.
                    Unlike
neighbors gone south for sun
and surf, I chose as always
to stay.
          But winter—the winter
I expected—never happened.
Robins returned in February
   and never left.
              Irises and tulips
   bloomed and kept blooming.
Relieved of shoveling and snow-
   blowing, I felt selectively
   lucky although I knew
   that happiness based on luck
   lessens always back to fact.
Instead, I bore the guilt
   by being totally prepared
   for everything but being spared.

Buried at Sea

It's not forgiving.
                    Surging
   or settled, its threats
   can be fatal.
                    Earth and air
   await our footsteps or drawn
   breaths, but the sea threatens.
Guards, boats and jackets,
   when prefixed by life, prepare
   to save us from the final gulp
   and swallowing if possible.
Wakened by nightmares, we sit
   upright and shivering like victims
   spared the slowest of drownings.
Tsunamis, floods and tidal
   waves endanger millions
   while a dead calm conceals
   riptides and coral reefs.
Signs of the sinkable or drowned
   litter the basement of the sea
   that waits for others to sail
   or swim just far enough
   to tire and panic and fail.

Reveille

Asleep and trapped, you dream
   what never dared to happen
happen.
          Sentenced to nightmares
of grief, shock or extinction,
there's no defense.
               Waking
is the last and only freedom
left that lets you bless
each breath you take to pad
your yearly spins around
the sun.
          But what's the point?
Numbered or not, the years
   add up to now.
          Beyond
mortality, the sun shines on,
and life still happens when all
that happened once is gone.

In Concert

"Music may be the ultimate art, but a
woman's voice is the ultimate music."
                              —*Overheard remark*

A soprano sang an audience
        to silence.
                Every woman and some men
        dabbed eyelashes before
        they applauded and applauded...
Applauders of Caruso, Bjorling,
        Gigli or Pavarotti would have
        clapped no differently though not
        in tears.
                But arias by women
        like Albanese, Callas, Norman
        or de los Angeles touched
        the heart.
                It seems that something
        in a woman's voice subdues
        our hidden fears of being
        totally alone.
                This inspired
        thousands to offer one soprano
        the ultimate honor of tears.

The World of Four Chambers

"The heart has its reasons that the reason
cannot know."

—*Blaise Pascal*

"God is perceptible only in the heart."

—*Denis de Rougemont*

The heart speaks in all tongues
    but only with the eyes.
The last goodbyes are silent.
They weaken if written or spoken
    aloud.
            They are the only
language of the everlasting
now where those once
loved live on forever—
Mary Anne whose smile
made others smile—Bob
at home with the great books
and his favorite pipe—Kak
who proved that living for those
loved by choice is life
at its truest.
            It's best when least
acknowledged or never acknowledged
at all.
            If done for show,

34

it vanishes.

        I leave all true
believers to their shrines and holy
relics.

        Nothing's heard
or seen until the heart
reveals a world redeemed
each day without a word.

Within Earshot

A poem happens in pieces
    but with promise.
                 It
    orders you to put the pieces
    together until they say
    what you feel so others
    can feel the same.
                 It takes
    time or no time at all
    before a missing piece
    is suddenly there and waiting.
Poetry agrees to happen
    only when the poem's ready
    to be spoken.
                 After you hear it
    once, you keep on overhearing
    word after word after word.

Last Rights

My handwriting's illegible
    to everyone, including me.
At our fiftieth college reunion
    one classmate asked, "Weren't you
    Sam Hazo?"
                I'm
an inch shorter than I was
    three years ago.
                 My trousers
seem one size too large—
    my shoes one size too small.
I eat and drink much less
    than I should because I'm never
    that hungry or thirsty.
                Last week
I forgot my phone number...
                  Today
I threw a football thirty yards
    in a perfect spiral to my grandson.
And just like that I was twenty.

Undated

The statute of limitations varies
    for each of us, but death
    begins when breathing ends.
What never ends is anything
    said, sung, sculpted or written
    that's unforgettable—"He's
    with the ages now"—a Puccini
    aria sung by Jussi Bjorling—
    the head of the bestial Sphinx—
    the handwritten declaration
    penned by Jefferson.
                            Spoken,
    heard, made or read, they stay
    alive simply by staying alive.
Unlike believers who pray
    for immortality or the luck
    of the miraculous, the wise revere
    what lives beyond denial.
All that matters is endurance
    plus timing and emphasis.
It's like an Irish woman's
    answer when asked if she was
    who she was.
                    Instead of saying "Yes,"
    she said straightforwardly, "I am."
Which sounds more emphatic?

That's why I'm wary of those
    who base identity on rank,
    status or ancestry instead
    of self, talent and grit.
Becoming who we are
    or what we do by choice
    with no concern for fame
    is less a question than a quest.
When a name is spoken or a word
    written that lets perfection happen,
    nothing is ever the same.

Ends and Odds

So much appeals to appetite—
   not only food or flesh
   but wealth, triumph and power.
Locations range from battlefields
   to bedrooms.
                Captured in Egypt,
   the squat and scheming scion
   of Alexander the Great seduced
   both Caesar and Mark Antony.
At Waterloo, Napoleon's only
   victory was exile.
                Hitler's
   dream of world dominion
   ended in the snows of Stalingrad.
When more is never enough,
   desire demands still more
   but never blames itself.
Nothing lessens the lure
   of attraction.
                Because no power
   but power can cope with power,
   all hedonists deny denial.
They feel no shame or guilt
   when they are gratified.
They see what some would call

deceit as nothing but
attraction by another name.

Rex

If excellence means doing
   better what others merely
   do well or not at all,
   Ralston Milton Nettleford
   more than qualified.
                  As Rhodes
   Scholar, Vice-Chancellor
   and professor who loathed "degree
   factories," he was known
   to his fellow Jamaicans as Rex.
He had the ease of a friend
   and the poise of an ebony king.
Without an advance in funding
   he founded the Jamaica National
   Dance Theater Company.
"We have the bodies," he pledged,
   "and only our bodies—not funds—
   make dancing possible."
Famous soon beyond Jamaica,
   his company toured the world,
   fulfilling Derek Walcott's
   prophecy of the Caribbean's
   destiny, "We are a nation,
   or we are nothing."
                  On a par
   with Prime Minister Michael

Manley and Louise Bennett,
    Rex was the pride of the island.
Fame and thirteen honorary
    doctorates followed.
                    Honors
    for Rex were empty as applause—
    sincerely brief but vainglorious.
He made it his mission to see
    that all Jamaicans were given
    the chance to be entranced by African
    rhythms.
                These started slowly,
    then swelled in tempo and passion
    until the listener lived for nothing
    but dancing, dancing, dancing.

End of Argument

Aristotle and Camus believed
    that happiness was ours to find
    in wisdom, virtue and pleasure.
Somehow, they overlooked
    the influence of good or bad
    luck.
        Beyond anticipation
or control, luck interrupts
for better or worse our quest
for truth, goodness or health.
Whatever seems is seen as so...
After she reached one hundred
    on the Fourth of July, Eva
    Marie's birthday was old news...
Upon returning to Europe, a tourist
    was asked to name the saddest
    people he met at a circus.
   "Clowns," he said...
              Considered
lucky to have married a prince,
Grace Kelly said she wanted
nothing more than "a day off..."
Aging with his wounds and "not
    having it good in bed
    any more," Hemingway absolved
    himself in Idaho.

Because
all crimes are wrongs while not
all wrongs are crimes, he chose
self-murder as his final no.

It's Just a Game

What happens happens instantly
    or not at all.
                Time means
moving through space or waiting
to move.
              Each pitch leaves
both teams primed to create
a new game.
                 No pitch?
No game.
             Even prepared,
a batter will fail to hit
a pitched ball more than
seven out of ten times.
Players poise crouched
    at their positions.
                  Except
for first basemen, lefthanded
infielders are not on the roster.
Running counterclockwise
    from home to all the bases
    means zero compared to scoring.
The team that's ahead after
    nine innings wins.
                 If tied,
the teams play on and on.

Unless forfeited, it's unlikely
but possible that tied teams
could never stop playing.

Part III

A Song of Songs

Inspired by Umm Kulthum

I saw her filmed in concert
   singing "You Are My Life"
that could have been intended
for a person, a people or a country.
She sang the song with such
   passion it could have been all three.
It lasted longer than an hour.
An audience of thousands—mostly
   men—never stirred except
to applaud when they were deeply
moved...
               As a girl she'd sung
for tourists in Alexandria.
                       Years
later in her prime she sang
a different song monthly
by the Nile.
               Egyptians huddled
around their radios and listened.
Rumor had it that any
   Arab state would collapse
overnight if she were invited
to sing and declined.
               More

than four million attended
her funeral in Cairo...
                              On film
she stood erect, poised and totally
possessed by the music she seemed
to offer as a gift to her audience.
With just a smattering of Arabic
I barely understood a word.
When the eighty-minute song ended,
    most men in the audience stood
    and kept standing at attention
    while some seemed too transformed
    to move and still others wept.

In Perpetuity

Buried together in Alsace—
    she, first, with her full name—
    RAISSA MARITAIN—plus dates
    centered on the headstone—
    he, thirteen years later
    with dates below his name
    etched smaller than a postscript
    near the base—*Et Jacques.*

To Be Exact

Today is yesterday's tomorrow,
    which simply means that then
    becomes now over and over.
True lovers could care less.
The time of clocks and dates
    does not exist for them except
    as obstacles.
           All they want
is time to touch and be
alone together.
           Whatever
threatens to part them finally
or briefly makes dearer
the time they share.
           Consider
Juliet and Romeo, Roxanne
and Cyrano or Jack and Jill.
Nothing can part them
    as a pair.
           Nothing ever will.

Once for Two

A brief absence of one
   from the other imposes
   absence on them both.
Since presence is all that matters
   for each, their yesterquestions
   disappear.
             Fulfillment
   is total, which means a least
   noticed but genuinely chosen
   love will outlive all inborn
   love for kin, country or cult.
Predictably the last objections
   to authentic love will come
   from family, culture or religion.
Spurning alternatives or doubts,
   two lovers share a lifelong
   life in ways that neither
   can imagine.
             Without a need
   to say or see, there's nothing
   for them to do but be.

Wed

The sapling we planted thirty
    years ago umbrellas our home
    today.
          In fact, it's two trees
    fused at the trunk—almost
    a metaphor.
           Every April
    it blossoms white at the crown
    but pink on all the branches.
Totally symmetrical, it shows
    how nothing guarantees perfection
    but proportion.
           Grafted in place,
    our tree sustains the ultimate
    balance—one half wild cherry
    but bound at the root to whatever
    the other will turn out to be.

From This Life Forth

Even when asked, I never
   can recite in public any
   poem I wrote for you
   alone.
        Many of them
   are published in books, but saying
   them would choke me.
               Doctors
   told me to forget that crucial
   morning when you looked at me
   and asked, "Who are you?"
At that moment our medical
   and married lives clashed
   until you suddenly took
   my hand and said, "Sam,
   answer the phone."
           Only
   when I dream of you are we
   still one another's best.
It lets me wake believing
   that a life we chose together
   has outlived the life we're born
   to lose and always will.

After Death

Alone for years, I am halved—
    no one to have breakfast with,
    no one to kiss with both eyes
    closed, no one who could feel
    the pain of others as her own.
Sleeping side by side
    for decades makes sleeping now
    a challenge where dreams await
    with more ferocity than fact.
I often wake and walk
    and smoke my pipe until
    I calm.
            If union's only future
is reunion, what's left but hope
though hope's indefinite while love
is sure.
            Dead lovers by the trillions
would share the answer with us
if they could, but love's a vow
of silence born to testify
that love outlives the curse
of death but never why or how.

Distantly Near

Last night I reached for you
    and touched a blanket—just
    a blanket.
                Eight years ago
    you would have touched me back.
Some say the pain of losing
    one you love lessens
    over time.
                In fact, it widens
    and deepens.
                Lines from an old
    and even older poet frame
    the twin results of loss.
The first confesses, "I won't
    look at myself as I am,
    and can't see myself
    as I used to be."
                The other
    concludes, "We live by touch."

Out of Touch

"...caressing staves off something."
Rainer Maria Rilke

Deprived of touch, I let absence
    remember those I loved:
    my brother coping with being
    alone in Paris, Mary Anne
    teaching Sam to walk and spell
    his name, my Aunt Kak
    dousing an owl with dishwater.
Parted for years, I reach
    for them and touch nothing.
Feeling them near means everything
    when touching nothing is all
    that's left.
                I'm not the first
or last to say so.
                After
all caressing ends, the choice
of saying so on paper
with a pen does nothing more
than worsen my regret for all
that's over.
             I mull "the ruins

of experience" and learn
that what I feel means more
than all I know.
                Nothing
but the last embrace stays real.

Now Is Always Next

While most religions prophesy
    what's next as paradise, eternity,
    heaven and similar dreams,
    I think what's next should be
    a love that happens when chosen
    and shared.
                Based on what
    I've seen and heard, all those
    who love and are loved in return
    rarely find ways to explain
    just how that's so and why.
Love and love-in-waiting
    rhyme daily and beyond
    because each one reflects
    the other.
                Taken together,
    they make a fool of time.

SAMUEL HAZO

The author of over fifty books of poetry, fiction, essays and plays, Samuel Hazo is the founder of the International Poetry Forum in Pittsburgh, Pennsylvania. He is also McAnulty Distinguished Professor of English Emeritus at Duquesne University, where he taught for forty-three years. From 1950 until 1957 he served in the United States Marine Corps (Regular and Reserve), completing his tour as a captain. He earned his Bachelor of Arts degree magna cum laude from the University of Notre Dame, a Master of Arts degree from Duquesne University and his doctorate from the University of Pittsburgh. Some of his previous works are *The Less Said, The Truer* and *Becoming Done* (Poetry), *If Nobody Calls, I'm Not Home* (Fiction), *Tell It to the Marines* (Drama), *Entries from the Interior* and *Who Needs a Horse That Flies?* (Essays), *Smithereened Apart* (Critique of the poetry of Hart Crane), *The Pittsburgh That Stays Within You* (Memoir awarded the 2018 IPPY national bronze citation for creative non-fiction) and *The World Within the Word: Maritain and the Poet* (Critique). His translations include Denis de Rougemont's *The Growl of Deeper Waters*, Nadia Tueni's *Lebanon: Twenty Poems for One Love* and Adonis' *The Pages of Day and Night*. He has been awarded twelve honorary doctorates. He was honored with the Griffin Award for Creative Writing from the University of Notre Dame, his alma mater, and was chosen to receive his tenth honorary doctorate from the university in 2008. A National Book Award finalist, he was named Pennsylvania's first State Poet by Governor Robert Casey in 1993, and, refusing a salary, he served until 2003. For his lifetime work, he is the recipient of the 2024 Common Wealth Award for Literature.

www.ingramcontent.com/pod-product-compliance
Lightning Source LLC
Chambersburg PA
CBHW032028090426
42741CB00006B/779